What's My Guinea Pig?

A Guide to Guinea Pig Breeds

Peter Gurney

Contents

Foreword

I was around eight years old when I bought my first guinea pigs. They were three in number and I christened them Pip, Squeak and Wilfred after some strip cartoon characters who were popular at the time. It turned out that in one respect at least I had been sold a pup or, to be more precise, a sow. One morning, before going to school, I went to give them their breakfast and, to my utter astonishment, lo and behold!: there were three tiny newcomers sharing the hay. Lessons received scant attention that day. I couldn't wait to get back home and take a closer look.

In those days I didn't have Peter Gurney to advise me. Peter would have put me right long before the event, but at that time I could scarcely believe my eyes. Small though they were, they were complete in every respect - whiskers, fur, squeaks - and from the look on their faces all three were clearly wondering what was for supper. Guinea pigs start as they mean to go on; what you see from the word go is the pig, the whole pig and nothing but the pig.

After a gap of many years I bought another for my daughter, Karen. Olga da Polga came from a pet shop in Basingstoke and cost four shillings and sixpence in what my mother would have called real money (now 22½p). She soon settled down as one of the family and after a while I began writing stories about her. It was a bit of a challenge at first because spending most of her time in a hutch as she did meant the sort of adventures that befall most other animals were denied her. But that didn't stop her fantasising and making up her own tales, which were duly passed on.

There was another long gap before Olga II arrived on the scene. In the fullness of time she died and the house seemed empty without her, so Olga III took over our lives. She was different again, for no two guinea pigs are ever the same; each has its own individual character. She was brave where Olga II had been nervous and she soon had the house organised as she wanted it to be. Then, when she was about three years old, we became worried because she seemed to have gone off her food - a state of affairs which, as far as guinea pigs are concerned, is always a cause for alarm, for they are basically eating machines. Something had to be done, and a telephone call to the Cambridge Cavy Trust put us in touch with Peter Gurney.

Peter lives, breathes and devotes his life to what he calls 'his guineas'. Anyone who can share a room with around 80 and not only know them all by name but also be conversant with their individual likes and dislikes, their fancies and their foibles, has to be someone special, and Peter is just such a person. He doesn't hang about; before Olga had time to say,

'Watch what you're doing!' her heart and various other organs had been checked and pronounced in good working order. Her lungs were clearly functioning well. Squeaks of outrage came from the patient as she suddenly realised that while she wasn't looking all her toe-nails had been cut.

Olga da Polga.

Having given her the once-over, Peter took her off her daily regime of pills and creams and antibiotics (all of which were costing us a small fortune) and prescribed instead a dab of this and a touch of that; old-fashioned remedies with a familiar ring. We left with strict instructions to come back in two or three days if they didn't work, but they did. In no time at all Olga was a new pig; on her feet again and busily making up for lost time.

Until then all our guinea pigs had been Abyssinian, largely because as a breed they are, so to speak, thicker on the ground; but also because we have naturally gravitated towards them for sentimental reasons. Our visit to Peter opened a door onto a whole new world. As newcomers to guinea pigs will discover from this book, they come in many different shapes, sizes and configurations and are called after various parts of the globe. Fortunately, aside from his talents as a guinea pig guru, Peter Gurney is no mean photographer and the combination of the two makes for thoroughly delightful viewing as well as reading.

Michael Bond

Introduction

One of the questions I am most often asked is, 'What kind of guinea pig do I have here?' The aim of this book is to enable people to work it out for themselves and to make them aware that the mixed breeds are as wonderful as their classier relations. Although this book includes the show standard guinea pig stars it is mainly about those that do not reach the grade: the mongrels, if you like.

Another question I am very often asked is, which is my favourite of all my guinea pigs, and I always reply that it is the one I happen to have in my arms at the time. Yet another common question is, which breed do I prefer. If pushed, I will go for the long-haired coronets. However, I always lack conviction when I give this reply, feeling that in so doing I am being unfaithful to all the other breeds.

My problem is that I have never met a guinea pig that I didn't like, even those who have bitten me or emptied both their bladders and bowels upon me! This love affair of mine, with a species to which the human race owes so much and for which it has done so little in return, started in middle age and will end only when they nail me down in my little wooden box. I am not expecting there to be a hereafter but, if there is and I find myself reunited with the many guinea pigs whose leaving of this life has caused me to shed so many tears, I shall be delighted to have had it wrong all those years. However, eternity will still not be long enough for me to give back to them all that they have given to me. What life I have left will be devoted, as it has been since the first one trotted into it and carved its name in a corner of my heart, to the improvement of the husbandry and veterinary care of these gentle, adorable creatures.

Since these animals came into my life, they have introduced me to some wonderful human beings which, considering how wary I have always been of this particular species, is a pretty neat trick! The fact that there are so many of them is particularly pleasing, as is the certainty that their numbers are increasing, for I believe that the ownership of guinea pigs has a great civilising influence on the 'wild' human being.

For quite a few years now I have been visiting Great Ormond Street Children's Hospital with my guinea pigs, but I regard this activity more as a self-indulgence than an act of good work. To see a sick child with one of my guinea pigs snuggled up in his or her lap, feeding it from the 'guinea pig take-away box', is a pleasure for which there is no price tag. Perhaps therein lies the answer to yet another question: 'Why do you love guinea pigs so much?' I know exactly how a child feels with that small bundle of warmth in its lap: protective and very privileged to have its trust. That is precisely how I feel, and for a 56-year-old man to be able to experience the same feeling, for the same reason, at the same time as a child just has to be something very special.

I would like to thank Myra Mahoney, Vice-President of The Peruvian Cavy Club of Great Britain, for technical advice, and Colin Jeal for photographing the show cavies and rare breeds.

Chapter 1 The Abyssinian

A show quality Brindle Abyssinian.

The most distinguishing features of this breed are the tufty whirls and curls that make up most of the coat, forming ridges where their outer diameters meet. These whirls and curls are called rosettes. At shows, points are awarded for good depth radiating from pin-point centres of the rosettes, which should be distributed symmetrically over the body. There should be a back ridge across the spine, just forward of the back legs, then a centre ridge running fore and aft up the spine, followed by a collar ridge that runs into the mane over the top of the head. Ridges should be proud and erect, and these too should be symmetrical, the cross one at right angles to the fore and aft ones. Under the lower jaw there should be a bristly moustache. The mane should be pronounced and the moustache prominent. The coat should have good depth and be harsh to the touch. It should be lustrous, with clear, bright colours. The body should be thick-set, of a cob shape, broad at the shoulder and substantial. The eyes should be big, bold and bright, and the ears large and drooping.

All guinea pig breeds can be subdivided into their various colours and coat textures, adding up to a veritable galaxy of guinea pig varieties, and additional points can be earned in these categories.

Abygale, pictured below, is a perfect example of a Tricolour Abyssinian show standard cavy. She has a lovely rough-textured coat, well pronounced rosettes and fine rose-petal ears.

One of the most affectionate guinea pigs I have ever owned was an Abyssinian called Becky, pictured on page 10. She was a Tricolour brought to me after her owner had died. She was certainly not a perfect specimen of the breed, and was no spring chicken when I took her on. However, she lived for a further three years, reaching an estimated age of seven, which is pretty good for a guinea pig.

One of the least affectionate, at least towards me, was Madame Bom-bom, the beautiful white beast shown on page 11, whose face and part of whose back turned dark grey as she advanced in years. This is not uncommon in white guinea pigs. Similarly, cream cavies tend to get areas of dark buff with age, particularly on their backs.

In truth, only the Bombom's head could really be classed as Abyssinian, and even that was rather 'iffy', as it had a lopsided coronet on it. There was certainly a large dash of Sheltie in the rest of her body, which ironed out most of the rosettes.

Whenever I picked

Abygale the Abyssinian: a lovely Tricolour.

Madame Bom-bom up and tried to 'nose-nuzzle' her, she would strain away from me with an expression upon her face as though there was something definitely distasteful under her delicate, pretty little nose. Despite all my efforts, she remained aloof and very distant, even after living with me for six years. Needless to say, the more this little lady resisted me, the more I loved her!

One group of Abyssinian cross-breeds has come by common consent (though not by the cavy fancy) to be classed as a separate breed, the Ridgeback. These guinea pigs are mainly smooth-coated but, beginning in the middle of the back, the hair becomes whirly

or simply sticks up, converging to a narrow ridge along the top of the spine. From here it runs to the top of the head, coming to a point between the ears, or sometimes forward of them, then curling to one side like a 1950s Teddy boy's quiff.

Dandy, a magnificent boar of mine, was a prime example of a Ridgeback. As can be seen by his picture on the opposite page, if ever a guinea pig was accurately named, he was. Watching him strutting his stuff in front of the glass front of my living-room pen,

Becky: not a show specimen, but one of the most affectionate cavies I've ever known.

home to 15 sows, you needed very little imagination to add a pair of blue suede shoes, shoulder pads, a string tie - and he already had the flashy waistcoat in the pattern of his coat!

Last, but by no means least, there is Olga da Polga - yes, *the*

Olga da Polga: a true leading lady.

Olga, heroine of Michael Bond's children's books. The man himself arrived at my door one day a couple of years back, having been referred to me by the Cambridge Cavy Trust.

All I knew was that a certain Mr Bond was bringing his guinea pig to me because she was off colour and, even when he said her name was Olga, I did not make the connection. Only when I showed him my book *The Proper Care of Guinea Pigs*, and he said that Olga was the guinea pig heroine I had referred to in that, was there a heavy clunking sound in my brain as the proverbial penny finally dropped. Needless to say, I was on tenterhooks until Michael

Madame Bom-bom: Madame by name and madam by nature.

telephoned a few days later to say that Olga was much better after the course of medicine I had prescribed for her. The thought of failing this, of all guinea pigs, had been daunting in the extreme. I'm sure that, had I failed, Vedra Stanley, founder of the Cambridge Cavy Trust, would have given me a loaded revolver and told me to go out and do the decent thing!

I am pleased to say that this famous and very self-assertive little lady has now become a regular boarder with me whenever the Bonds go on holiday.

Dandy the Ridgeback: a perfect example of a 1950s 'Ted'.

Chapter 2 The Agouti

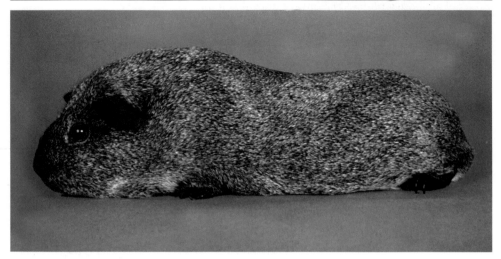

Show quality Silver Agouti.

The easiest way to describe an Agouti's coat is to say that it is like that of the common English rabbit. The highlighting, or ticking as it is known in the show world, is caused by each individual hair being lighter at the tip than at the shaft. Show quality Agouti guinea pigs should not have eye circles, broken coat (that is, uneven distribution of colour), side whiskers, excessive white hairs in the body hair or odd white feet. All these are considered faults. Standard show colours for Agoutis are Golden, Silver, Cinnamon, Chocolate, Lemon and Cream.

- The Golden Agouti, much to my puzzlement, has to be a dark mahogany colour, not in the least bit golden!
- The Silver Agouti really does look silver. The best show quality Silvers have rich black hair shafts, with very light grey tips. This is what gives the animal such a true silver sheen.
- The Cinnamon Agouti is a very light brown colour, almost orange, like the spice. The ticking does not seem as pronounced on these because the underlying colour of the hair shafts is quite light.
- The Chocolate, Lemon and Cream Agoutis are all self-explanatory.

On show quality animals, the belly colour should be very much lighter than the rest of the coat, and there should be a very clear line of demarcation where the topside and underside meet.

The name 'Pearl' instantly springs to mind whenever I see an Agouti guinea pig. She was the first Agouti I owned, and a strong factor in my good opinion of Agoutis is undoubtedly the fact that she was a very gentle little creature who had the ability to capture the hearts of all those who met her. In cavy show ring terms she was flawed because she had a small white patch on her back and the area around her eyes was much lighter than the rest of her coat. The owner of the pet shop where I bought her, who does not normally stock guinea pigs, said she was a reject from a show breeder: hence her cheapness at £2.

Little Pearl repaid my modest investment by giving me six years of her delightful company. She never had a day's ill health and died the way she had lived: quietly and with gentle dignity. During the last week of her life I supplemented her food by feeding her by syringe, as she had too little energy to feed herself. She would come to the front of her pen and make piping noises whenever she was ready to eat. Since that time I have observed this behaviour in quite a few guinea pigs who have died natural deaths. Then the day arrived when she stuck her head in a corner of her pen, turning her back on her companion and the world: a sure sign that a guinea pig has decided it is time to go.

The light rings around gentle little Pearl's eyes stopped her from being a show girl.

Later that evening she came to the front of the pen and piped once more. Thinking that perhaps she had changed her mind about that final journey I made up some more food for her, which she promptly refused. Puzzled, I put her down again, only to hear her piping as soon as I turned to go back into the kitchen. She had always enjoyed her bread and milk, particularly the milk, lapping it up around the bits of bread before tucking in. I made up a small dropper bottle of warm milk, wrapped Pearl in a towel and, by the light of my bedside lamp, sat with her in my arms while she greedily guzzled two-thirds of the bottle before being sated. I remember thinking that she had come into this life sucking from her mother and now she was leaving it sucking from me. There was a beautiful kind of symmetry to it all, and I felt very privileged to be included in her dying as I had been in all of her living.

Having performed the last duty I owed her, I put her back into her self-selected corner, and the following morning there she lay, quite dead. Although I had expected just that, tears welled up in my eyes, as they were to do for so many more guinea pigs to whom I have had to say goodbye.

Arthur, pictured opposite, is a fine example of a Golden Agouti. Apart from a slightly wavy ear on one side, he scores in every way. The coat is superb, being of an even colour all over with no lighter rings around the eyes.

Arthur the Golden Agouti shows off his beautiful, even coat.

Flickie comes from a long line of heavy guinea pigs. Her grandson is certainly carrying on the tradition, weighing in at 1.4kg (3lb) at only eight months old. However, none of her family can be considered overweight: they are all big-framed, carrying proportionally less weight than many of their smaller companions. Flickie gets her name partly in honour of a friend of mine called Felicity and partly because she has some long hair on her rump that flicks upwards, which would certainly disqualify her from competition in the Agouti class.

Dennis and Dusty, two litter-brothers who are among the most amicable boars I have ever known, are examples of the ultimate mix. Their basic coat colour is a mixture of golden and lemon, and even this mix is uneven. Dusty has a part-bib of white under his chin and a white dash over his left ear, while his brother has a band of brown around the middle of his body. These two characters have a habit of leaning over the top of the glass front of their pens whenever I have visitors. There they

Flickie is large for a guinea pig.

perch like a pair of country yokels chewing the fat and putting the world to rights. Needless to say, they have a great fuss made of them and receive plenty of titbits for this 'trick' - something they obviously worked out a long time ago!

Of the two of them, Dennis is the more adventurous, and it nearly cost him his life one day when they were on a free-range expedition. I was cleaning the main sow pen when the sack in which I was collecting the soiled hay and newspaper slipped down onto the floor. A little while afterwards I picked it up again, without thinking anything about it. Three hours later, when I went to put the brothers back into their quarters - no Dennis!

Dennis and Dusty: a pair of country yokels putting the world to rights!

It didn't take me long to work out what had happened but, rushing out to the dustbin, I found to my horror that it had been filled up with building rubble. Laying the bin on its side, very gingerly I began to take everything out. To my great relief, about two thirds of the way down the two-metre bin I saw a familiar face staring at me accusingly. Needless to say, I now check my sacks very carefully after I have mucked out!

Generally speaking, I do not think character traits are determined by particular breeds. I would make an exception of Agoutis, however, whom I consider to be no-nonsense, feet-firmly-on-the-ground characters. I have yet to come across one who is scatty, and most people who have owned them assure me that their experience is identical to my own.

15

Chapter 3 The Crested

A show quality Golden American Crested.

There are two basic types of Crested guinea pigs: the American and the English. As the names suggests, each type has a crest on the crown of its head. The English has a crest in the same colour as that of its coat, while the American has a crest in a contrasting colour, usually white. Cresteds can include Himalayan, Agouti, Dutch, Tortoiseshell-and-white, Dalmatian and Roan, whereas

Father and son: Basil (above) and Barnaby (above right).

the American type is restricted to Selfs (guinea pigs with a coat of only one colour).

The same basic rules of uniformity of coat, large wide eyes, well-defined ear flaps and short cobby bodies with deep broad shoulders that apply to all show guinea pigs are relevant to the Crested. The crest of a show animal should radiate from a well-defined centre point between the eyes and ears, with the lower edge well down the nose.

What I like about these animals is the jaunty air the crest seems to give them. I think I prefer the American because the different colour of the crest from the rest of the body gives the animal more razzmatazz.

Basil, my Cream American Crested cavy lives with his son Barnaby, a White English Crested. While Basil can be a little intolerant of human handling, Barnaby simply adores humans. When you cradle him in your arms you have an animal in his seventh heaven. Someone once remarked of Barnaby that he's so laid back that he's almost horizontal!

Barnaby has had fatty eye, a droopy lower eyelid condition relatively common in guinea pigs, since he was about six months old. This occurs more often in elderly guinea pigs, but is not a danger to their health, although cavies with this problem are automatically disqualified from the show ring. Most people assume that Barnaby is much older than his 18 months because of his deliciously droopy eyes. They give him a sad, puppy-dog-lost look, and I too find it very hard not to pick him up and hug him whenever I'm passing.

Freda: a chip off the old block in appearance and character.

17

Barnaby's sister, Freda, takes after their father; she is a typical American Crested, her crest being a particularly pronounced one, as you can see in the picture on page 17. She also takes after her father in nature, not sharing her brother's love of humans at all, although she was a wonderfully caring and attentive mother to her litter of four.

Bobby has 'dual nationality' - just a few white hairs in his crest.

Bobby is a mixture of English and American Crested. His crest has many white hairs in it, but the rest of it is the same Silver Agouti as his body. He is about four years old now, and has all the Agouti steadiness that I have come to expect.

Blossom, one of the prettiest guinea pigs I have ever owned, is the ultimate Crested mongrel. The colour patterning on her coat is Dutch (see chapter 5) but has gone slightly awry. Her crest, though wonderfully wide, has white hairs running into the white patch on the back of her neck. For me, those deep, dark eyes make her a pedigree from the very top drawer, but even when they are tightly closed she is what the word *cute* is meant to mean! When she was brought to

Blossom: one of the prettiest guinea pigs I've ever owned.

me by a friend she was only six months old and had already had two litters, both of which had caused her problems. Although I would love to continue her line, the inconsiderate behaviour of her last owner in allowing her to get pregnant twice at such an early age obliges me to forgo the pleasure of producing more little Blossoms.

Chapter 4 The Coronet

A show quality Coronet groomed ready for the ring.

This is the first long-haired breed to be mentioned, and a particular favourite of mine. My current free-range guinea pigs are particularly fine examples of this breed. They are litter brothers called Dodson and Horrell, and I shall write more about them later.

The coronet on the heads of these guinea pigs is like an over-emphasised crest. The longer hair gives it more of a fountain effect as it cascades down over the ears and shoulders. For show purposes it has to be neat, even and symmetrical, so the cascading must not be over-done. For my taste, the more the coronet flows about the head and shoulders, the better I like it.

In a show quality Coronet it is important that the head is nice and broad with wide-spaced, large eyes. I can certainly see the point of this: the coronet needs the wide spread of a broad head to be displayed to advantage. The coat must be of good texture with a good density all around. It should sweep the

Mr Chipper: a noble head and deportment to match.

Dodson posing for the camera.

ground and not have any eddies of upturned hair to spoil the line. There should be a clearly-defined parting of hair running up the spine.

Mr Chipper (page 19) was probably the most aristocratic guinea pig I ever owned. He was a perfect tricolour, with a noble head and a deportment to match. He never just walked into a room: he made an entrance, with an imperious air that made those already there feel that some kind of obeisance was in order. I adored Mr Chipper, and was devastated when he died prematurely at the age of two-and-a-half of a torsion of the gut. That the publisher of my first book also recognised his outstanding beauty, using his image again and again, speaks volumes for the presence he had, even in his photographs.

Dodson could make it into the show ring with a bit of trimming up and tidying, but his brother could not. Everything about Doddy, as I call him, is there: carriage, colours and coronet. His temperament is certainly suited for showing, for he is always at his ease with humans. This quality is important with pet show judges and can earn extra points.

Dodson and Horrell came to me from a family in which one of the children developed an allergic reaction to their hair. This kind of allergy is more common in the case

Dodson and Horrell: always the best of friends.

20

of animals with thick, luxuriant fur, like cats, but I have come across it before; a friend of mine adored Mr Chipper but, unfortunately, would come out in a skin rash after just a few minutes of close contact with him.

Dodson and Horrell are the first pair of boars I have allowed to run free range in my home. I have always been cautious about having free-range boars in pairs with so many pens containing sows at ground level. Some of these sows are outrageous flirts, hooking their forepaws over the top of the glass fronts of their pens, wriggling their bottoms and purring seductively at any boar in sight. I thought that such behaviour was bound to cause friction between a pair of boars vying for their favours but, though the brothers respond enthusiastically, I have yet to see any sign of aggression between them. Quite the reverse, in fact: they seem to be sexually ambivalent! Once passions have been aroused from their close encounters with the sows they will leap on

Free Range Fred: the ultimate *Heinz 57*.

and off each other's backs with great eagerness. However, they never let their desire overcome their good manners for, no matter how heated they are, they always seem to display what I can only describe as consideration and courtesy towards each other.

Finally, there is Fred, who is a real mixture. I think he has equal amounts of Coronet, Sheltie and Peruvian. I get many letters from kind people who liked my last book and all, without exception, ask after Fred, the famous free-ranger. As can be seen from the picture above, he would not get a look-in as a show quality Coronet. There is the residue of a coronet under the small scruff of hair that lops over his forehead but that's about all. Some of the hair of his coat lies forward, in the manner of a Peruvian, some backwards, like a Sheltie.

Fred came to me with kidney problems and only lived for a further 18 months but, when his time came, I knew that my commitment to these adorable creatures was total. I shall always be grateful to him, not only for the very great pleasure of his company, but also for teaching me so much about his species.

Chapter 5 The Dutch

A show quality Dutch.

After the single-coloured Self, the Dutch must be about the most popular of all guinea pigs. However, to qualify for show standard it has to adhere to some very strict specifications.

Panda pig is my nickname for this breed, for the markings are very similar to those of a giant panda.

The coat is white, but with large patches of colour over the cheek, eyes and rump. The recognised colours are Black, Cream, Chocolate, Red, Cinnamon Agouti, Golden Agouti and Silver Agouti. The cheek markings must not cover the moustache pads and must be evenly balanced to leave a symmetrical blaze down the

Tubbit: a confident, self-assertive character.

Topsy and Tina would not win breed rosettes,
but they know they're beautiful.

snout. The ears must be the same colour as the patches, and flesh marks can lose points. As in the case of the Agouti standard guinea pig, eye circles in Dutch Agoutis are penalised. The rear feet must have white stops that do not go up to the hocks. In other words, it must look as though they are wearing pairs of socks without heels. The line of the colour that covers the rump must end around the middle of the body and be straight and even all the way round. The coat faults are the same as those in the Self standard: ruffles, whirls, rosettes, side whiskers and uneven coat.

Tubbit (below left) is a prime example of a magnificent Red Dutch. I often see him because he boards with me regularly when his owners go on holiday. He is confident, self-assertive and a very positive character. If you try to trim his claws when he is not in the mood he will show his assertiveness by doing his very best to bite your fingers. He is the kind of guinea pig with whom you simply do not take liberties; if you do, you must expect to pay the penalty.

Topsy and Tina do not quite make the grade as show girls. For a start, there is a flash of pink skin on Tina's left ear and she has an irregular eye patch on that side. Topsy has a similar flash on her right ear and both her eye patches are uneven and pointed. Both have proper 'white socks' on the rear feet: the trouble is, they only have one each!

Sarah, on page 24, would not stand the slightest chance of Dutch classification as far as show standard is concerned. Her coat is too long and, as she is Agouti, it is clear that the rings around the eyes let her down. The eye patches have extended to cover the whole of her head, leaving only a wonky blaze down the front of her snout. She has no socks at all and there is a patch of white on her rear end.

Betty on page 24 is barely recognisable as a Dutch. The flash down her snout is not too bad but the eye patches take the whole of her lower jaw and the one on the right extends down onto the side. From there, the white base colour covers the whole of the

Sarah would have no chance of winning classification as a show Dutch.

rump. On the other side, the rump colour extends too far up towards the head. This colour, which was once cream, is now a dull dun stretching over onto the back, with a fair amount of black in it. This is a fine example of a coat changing colour with age. In my experience,

about half my stock undergo this change, which can also occur in animals that have had a serious skin problem which has caused hair loss for a prolonged period of time.

This complete mix is so common that I sometimes think it is almost a breed in itself. I often refer to these pigs as *Dollies*, derived from Dolly Mixture sweets.

Betty's darker patches were once cream, but they have turned dun with age.

Chapter 6 The Himalayan, Standard and Crested

A show quality Himalayan.

The most common remark made by people when they see a Himalayan guinea pig for the first time is: 'Oh, it looks like a Siamese cat!' This is because of the black or chocolate nose, ears and feet in a coat that is otherwise pure white. The dark areas are called *pointing*.

Unlike the Dutch, whose 'socks' must stop well short of the ankle, the Himalayan must carry its 'socks' well up the leg. The colour of the ears must be dense right down to the base. The eyes should be large and a bright red. The coat must be smooth, free from any body stain and as white as possible. Brindling in any of the points is considered a fault, as is muddy body colour. White toe-nails, white patches on foot pads and white side whiskers disqualify this breed from the show standard. The colour of the smut should not appear anywhere else on the body.

The same basic rules apply for the Crested Himalayan, whose crest should be as near as possible to a complete circle.

I am always torn in two when confronted with one of these creatures. Part of me gets the giggles, for it seems to be trying to pull off the elegant aloofness of the Siamese cat. However, the stubby round body and short little legs of the guinea ensure that there is no way it can achieve this. Nevertheless, there is a touch of elegance about them and one with a very docile temperament certainly does have a regal air.

Horlic (right) is a fine example of a show standard Chocolate Himalayan. The smut (patch of chocolate) over her nose is nice and symmet-

Horlic, a Chocolate Himalayan.

rical and the ears uncrinkled. This guinea pig, one of my regular boarders, has the carriage of a lady of distinction, which would help her to win extra points in the show ring. If asked to describe characteristics like this I would find it hard to give a clear definition. I guess I would just have to say that a guinea pig either has it or it hasn't! A good show judge would notice it immediately, as would anyone wise in the ways of guinea pigs.

Heidi (left) was as near perfect as it is possible to get were it not for the slight crinkle in her ears and some white hairs on her back feet. She, too, had been a regular boarder with me all her life, living with three companions of

Heidi: almost perfect by show standards, quite perfect to her owner.

similar age. Her death was premature and, though I boarded her companions for some time afterwards, her little face was very conspicuous by its absence.

Yogi, the Crested Himalayan, is let down by the light shade of his smut and the white hairs on his back feet. This is a great pity, for the crest is one of the most beautifully formed I have ever seen on a guinea pig of any kind.

Yogi the Crested Himalayan proudly bears an exceptionally beautifully formed crest.

Chapter 7 The Peruvian

A show standard Peruvian.

This long-haired variety is the one that many people describe as the Dougal Dog, after the character on *The Magic Roundabout*. Its coat is certainly just like that of Dougal, who seems to be based on a Skye Terrier. The hair grows forwards towards the head from about half way down its body length rather than away from it, like all other varieties.

Willie, on the opposite page, was another of my few pure-breds. I am sure he would have won many prizes if I had exhibited him, for he met all the criteria for a show quality Peruvian. He had a very broad head with prominent eyes, and his fringe covered his face, although I seldom let it hang there when I photographed him as he had very expressive eyes. The fringe hung down each side of the head like a lion's mane, conforming to show standard quality. His coat was silky and very dense and long. To keep him tidy, I had to trim the fringe of the coat constantly, and this would have rendered him unfit for show standard as the coat must be permitted to grow long. As I never show my pigs I could allow myself the luxury of layer-cutting the hair on Willie's rear end, but I seldom had to trim the sides of the coat. As in most long-haired varieties, it flicked up off the ground and Willie kept it amazingly clean with constant grooming.

Willie's premature death at the age of about four came as a great blow to me and to the many human friends who made up his fan club. Never having had any kind of illness all his life, he went down suddenly with a respiratory infection and was dead within a week. Two other guinea pigs went down with the same problem at the same time. Both were older and in far less prime condition, but both survived. These circumstances reinforce a conclusion reached by many people, myself included, who study the health of small animals: that it is probably more healthy for an animal to be ill now and again to build up its reserves for when a more serious infection comes along.

Alex, pictured on page 30, is the great-grandson of Mr Chipper, mentioned in chapter 4. This merely proves that I have had two show standard Peruvians, and he is simply too beautiful to be left out! He is a classic example of a Tricolour, and the colours clearly indicate the family connection with Mr Chipper. He is a casual kind of a chap, laid back and, much to my chagrin, rather lazy in his stud duties. I am hoping that, at one year old, he is a late starter, but I suspect it could be something to do with a low sperm count. When he does rouse himself, his libido certainly seems to be as good as that of any other boar I have owned.

Willie: one of my few pure-breds.

Alex, great-grandson of Mr Chipper.

I cannot leave out my favourite sow, Katie, his mother. She too is a classic prize Peruvian sow, and a spirited wench, which is my polite way of saying that she is an out-and-out madam. She is given to fits of temper when one of her sister sows happens to look at her in the wrong way, and woe betide any boar who does not court her, and for a considerable length of time, before trying to mate with her. I remember wincing when once she head-butted a boar who tried to do it his way instead of hers.

Katie, a spirited wench.

Vedra, named after the founder of the Cambridge Cavy Trust.

Vedra (above), named after the founder of the Cambridge Cavy Trust, is fine as far as she goes, but is let down by the fringe, which parts either side of her head, and a bit of a whirl on her rump, indicating some Abyssinian in her lineage.

Pauline is simply a 'pick-and-mix' Peruvian. The fringe goes across the top of the head in much the same way as the fringe of a man with a receding hairline who is desperate to cover his deficiency. What her rump shows is anyone's guess: a mixture of Sheltie, Peruvian, Abyssinian and Uncle Tom Cobbleigh and all. As a nurse she would have been ideal - she recently underwent surgery for a urethral stone, and she neatly took out all her stitches three times afterwards!

Pauline, the 'pick-and-mix' Peruvian.

Chapter 8 The Rex

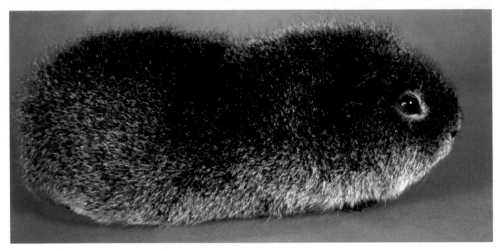

A show quality Rex.

I feel a tinge of sadness when writing about this breed for I recently lost my lovely Teddy Teddimus. He was the successor to the famous Free Range Fred and, at two-and-a-half years, his death was premature.

As Teddy's name suggests, he and all of his kind have what I can only describe as teddy-bear coats. The breed is called *Teddy* in America, and very appropriate it is.

The show standard demands a coat that is thick, short and springy. The springiness is caused by each individual hair being 'crimped', giving it more elasticity than is normal for guinea pig hair. The coarseness is more important on the back, while the sides and belly are allowed to be softer in texture. Points are deducted for extreme centre-parting, coat length greater than 1.3cm (half an

Teddy Teddimus was a real character who certainly didn't suffer fools gladly.

inch) and flatness of coat anywhere on the body. The rules of broad snouts, large, well-spaced eyes and good drooping ears apply to the Rex as they do to most other show guinea pigs.

Teddy Teddimus, whose picture appears on page 32, must be the most photographed of all my guinea pigs. If anything, he was even more self-assertive than Fred and, during the 18 months I had him, he stamped his personality very firmly in my home. Although the crinkly ears, slightly narrow snout and uneven coat ruled him out of the show standard, they didn't rule him out of my own and many other people's hearts, especially my mother's.

Tess is Teddy's *doppelganger* in appearance, but a pacifist by nature.

Teddy was a refugee whose previous owner said he was vicious, claiming Teddy had bitten both him and one of his sons. I never met this family but, having lived with the Teddimus, I'm sure he had a very good reason for biting them. He certainly didn't suffer fools gladly, and his definition of a fool was one who did not heed his warnings when he was not in the mood to be picked up or petted. I grew quite good at detecting these people as well. They were usually the ones who cried, 'Oh, he tried to bite me!' having been too stupid to heed his ample verbal warnings before he felt it necessary to resort to a more physical sanction in the shape of a pair of very efficient incisor teeth.

Saskia, pictured on page 34, has it all: lovely broad snout, thick springy coat, and large droopy ears. She is a gentle, motherly character. She lives in one of my main pens with 15 other sows and, if I introduce a 'minipig' recently weaned and missing its mother, it always seems to gravitate towards her. It will usually snuggle in close to her and be groomed and comforted.

Tess on page 33 is clearly Teddy's *doppleganger*, but only as far as appearance and faults against the show standard go. Whereas the Teddimus could be feisty and fierce, Tess is extremely laid back. No matter what the provocation, she either tucks her head well down and takes cover or strolls away with an air of total disinterest. This usually leaves the aggressor perplexed and with an expression of puzzlement on its face, wondering at the lack of response. It will then turn away, muttering to itself, and leave her alone - proving that young Tess is pretty shrewd in coming up with such an effective defensive technique.

Gentle, motherly Saskia looks after the 'minipigs' when I introduce them into the sow pen.

Chapter 9 The Satin

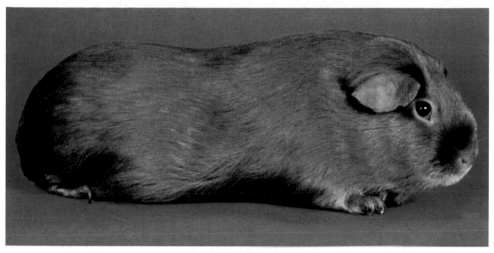

A show quality Golden Satin.

Chester has the good fortune to live in a pen with 17 sows.

The Satin is a guinea pig of any breed, but with a satin coat. The individual hairs have a glass-like quality, reflecting the light and giving the animal an enhanced sheen. The coat should be very fine, silky and evenly satinised all over. The show standard for any breed applies also to the Satins of that breed.

Chester, the magnificent White Satin pictured left, is a superb example of a show standard Satin. He has the great good fortune to live in a pen with 17 sows, as he is sterile. Although his libido is

35

as good as the next boar's he has been unproductive for the past two years and I sincerely hope he continues to be so. This isn't because I wouldn't want more of him; it is just that there would be so many more of him if he kicked into gear, so to speak, with so many sows available.

Chester has a lovely broad head, which he holds high, and his shoulders are substantial. As far as temperament is concerned, he is a pure 'pussy cat'.

Ginny's coat has the best sheen I have ever seen on a guinea pig. Pictured left, she is a Satin Lemon Agouti and, though she has never been shown, I'm sure she would come away with many rosettes if she were.

Ginny's coat has the best sheen I have ever seen on a guinea pig.

Albert (right) was a fine example of a show standard Satin Golden Sheltie, only slightly let down by some bumps in both his ear flaps. Sadly he died young, a fate which befalls quite a few Satins. The underlying cause is usually inbreeding, a practice to which I am very strongly

Albert, a handsome Satin Golden Sheltie.

opposed. It greatly weakens the animal's immune system and there is a greater incidence of dental problems with inbred Satins. I would never breed Satin to Satin, let alone two closely-related Satins.

Rusty, a delightful Crested Satin with a 'dual-nationality' crest.

Rusty is a delightful Crested Satin, a kind of American/English alliance in that her crest is half white and half the same colour as her body. This alone would disqualify her from the show circuit; add her low weight and tendency to 'bunny-hop' as she walks, and she is nowhere in the reckoning. I am particularly proud of this little lady because she was in an appalling condition when I acquired her; partly lame and with a colic that caused her to be constantly trying to find a comfortable position to lie in. I'm pleased to say that a combination of herbal and conventional medicine, plus lots of TLC, soon put her back on her feet, and now she can cope quite easily with the rough and tumble of living in one of my main pens with 18 other sows.

Chapter 10 The Standard Self

A show quality Cream Standard Self.

In essence, Standard Selfs are guinea pigs that are the same colour all over. Many people might think they own one, but there are many small points that can disqualify them.

The recognised colours for Standard Selfs are Black, White, Cream, Golden, Red, Chocolate, Beige and Lilac. The top coat must be very lustrous and of an even shade all over. The colour on the underside must match the top, and so must the hair on the feet. The coat must be short, with a nice sheen. The ears must be rose petal shaped, set wide apart and large and drooping. As with all show standard guinea pigs, the eyes should be large and bold.

Snowball, a particularly good example of a White Standard Self, can be seen in the picture on the opposite page. As you can see, her eyes are pink, but deep ruby or black eyes are also acceptable in a white. Helen's Choice (page 40), a Cream Self, is also definitely show class, with her nice coat, even all over, and her beautiful broad head.

Simon and Garfunkel (page 40), two magnificent boars of mine, had the desirable broad heads of show quality animals but were let down by the unevenness of their coats. They were 'almost' pigs in that one was almost cream and one almost gold, but neither quite! I always saw these two wonderful characters, who were litter-brothers, as perfect gentlemen. I took them on when they were about 18 months old and they lived with me for another five years. I did not see them have a disagreement in the whole of this time. Their manners were impeccable; when I dished out the evening carrot ration, one would wait patiently for his piece after his brother had been served. Not for them the statutory tug-o'-war or quick snatch and run favoured by most guinea pigs.

Hobbs, on page 41, is a typical example of a Self-that-isn't. The flash down the snout points to some Dutch lineage, while the rest of the body is pure Self. This different coloured flash can appear on other parts of the coat. I know of many cases where two apparently pure-bred Selfs produced a whole litter with this 'fault'. The only way you can have a reasonable chance of producing pure-bred guinea pigs of any type is to use those who have a long pure-bred lineage; that is, grandparents and great-grandparents of the same breed.

Wendy (page 41) was the ultimate mixed-breed Self. She was also one of the sweetest-natured animals I ever had.

Snowball, a Pink-eyed White Standard Self.

Helen's Choice, a Cream Self.

Whenever a new member was introduced to the sow pen and found herself the subject of the usual 'You're new, take that!' chin-butting that is part of the rough-and-tumble of pack life, she would seek refuge with Wendy. Wendy was not the least bit aggressive, but she was very large. Once a guinea pig had hidden behind her, pursuit would cease.

Simon and Garfunkel: beautiful heads, but let down by their uneven coats.

40

Hobbs: a typical example of the Self-that-isn't.

Wendy (right) sheltering a friend.

Chapter 11 The Sheltie

A show quality Sheltie.

The Sheltie is a Peruvian with a back-swept hairstyle. The flow of the hair is towards the rear of the animal, whereas on the Peruvian it flows forwards.

Like the Peruvian, the Sheltie has a natural parting down its spine, but this must not extend over the head. For show purposes, the hair should be the same length as the Peruvian's, growing at about 2.5cm (1in) a month.

Short-nosed and broad-headed, with large prominent eyes, the Sheltie is the debonair member of the long-haired varieties. The coat should be long, dense and silky in texture. In America the breed is referred to as the Silky. The sweep of the coat on the hindquarters is sometimes longer than on the sides.

Jilly (page 43), named after writer and journalist Jilly Cooper, was a case of almost-but-not-quite when it came to being a thoroughbred. She was the very first long-haired guinea pig I ever owned. I had been put off them because people had told me that the long-haired varieties were much harder to care for, needing more grooming and shampooing. While I agree that this is necessary for a show cavy, a long-haired pet guinea pig does not make much more work than a short-haired one. The main thing is to layer-cut the rear end to prevent soiling.

Jilly's biggest fault against the breed standard was in the parting in her mane, and her ears were a little too flat and not petalled. I fear there might have been a problem or two in temperament, as well. She was rather a feisty lady and, unless the judge had the ability to assess her qualities in five seconds flat, it would have been pointless to enter her - that was about the amount of time she would sit still.

Jilly, called after writer Jilly Cooper.

Jilly Cooper, being the kind of lady she is, carried on a correspondence with her small namesake throughout the five years of the latter's life. She informed her that she had had a racing car, a chrysanthemum and even a one-legged chicken called after her, but nothing quite as beautiful as Jilly-the-guinea! Obviously a lady of great taste and discernment.

Mungo's nose is a little too long and his eyes are not as prominent as they should be for show standard. His mane is not much to speak of and, though there is a kink in his ear, it is not what you would call petalled. However, he is a particularly gentle boar. When Buster, his Cream Rex pen-mate, was taken from his mother after weaning and put into Mungo's pen, he took one look at Mungo and began to squeak in alarm. Mungo responded by crouching low and gradually creeping forward, purring softly. When he was a few inches away from the now slightly calmer Buster he nuzzled him tentatively and then began to lick him around the ears. It was clear that, aware of the youngster's

Mungo, the gentle giant.

alarm, he was deliberately trying to allay his fears. This is not the sort of behaviour you expect from an adult boar at the introduction of a young one, the scent of its mother still heavy upon it.

Mindy is not quite sure what she is. For a start, she is far too small, and her head is that of a straightforward smooth-coated guinea pig. There is no parting down the spine, but there is definitely the skirt of a Sheltie. Some show standard guinea pigs look like this when they are born and quite a way on into their development, but this little lady was 18 months old when this photograph was taken.

Mindy is not quite sure what breed she is, but she knows she's lovely!

Chapter 12 Rare Breeds

Buffy, my Merino - the hair growth on her flanks looks like a Victorian lady's bustle.

Although this book is about popular breeds, I feel that there should be a chapter about the rarer breeds - most of which would probably be more popular with a little more publicity! One or two of the breeds in this chapter would not be regarded as all that rare by the cavy fancy. However, the vast number of people who keep guinea pigs entirely as pets would probably be unfamiliar with them.

For the past seven years my guinea pigs and I have been visiting the children at Great Ormond Street Children's Hospital. I regard these visits as a labour of love, even a self-indulgence, and they are certainly a good way of getting feed-back from the general public. One thing I have found out is that even the relatively common Sheltie or Peruvian has the average member of the public completely flummoxed.

'Goodness, I didn't know they had hair like that! They look more like Dougal dogs than guinea pigs,' is the most common response from nurse or parent when I place a representative of one of these breeds onto a child's bed.

I shall never forget the first time I took a Texel, a magnificent Chocolate boar, up to the hospital. As it happened, the first child I showed him to was surrounded, not just by one parent, but by what looked like a couple of aunts and uncles. Needless to say, the ham in me rose to the fore, and I hauled my new acquisition out of the travelling box with a very extravagant flourish. The OOhhs and AAhhs that my action provoked were most satisfying and I had great difficulty in restraining myself from topping things with an elaborate bow.

Wearing my Joe Public hat, I would list the rarer breeds as those in the table below. However, I would add the caution that breeding Dalmatians and Roans in particular should be left to the experts, as abnormalities and fatalities can result from breeding Roan to Roan or Dalmatian to Dalmatian.

• Alpaca	• Magpie
• Argenti	• Merino
• Bicolour	• Roan
• Brindle	• Texel
• Dalmatian	• Tortoiseshell-and-white
• Harlequin	

This is a mixed bunch of long-, short- and rough-coated guinea pigs. My particular favourite is the Merino, and I don't say that just because the example in this book happens to be one of my own guinea pigs. I didn't know they existed until a couple of years ago but, as soon as I set eyes on one at a show, I knew I just had to have one.

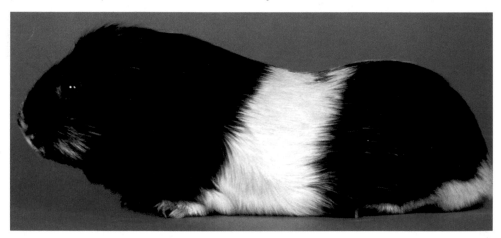

A Magpie.

Her name is Buffy and, as you can see from her picture on page 45, she has the same coronet as my favourite breed. What makes her such a perfect example of the breed is the hair growth on the flanks, which looks to me like the bustle that Victorian ladies wore. It

A young Alpaca, its hair not fully grown. An Alpaca could be described as a Rex Peruvian.

also happens to be the way the hair grows on the merino sheep, after which the breed is named.

I have only bred Buffy once, and shall not do so again. Although I was careful not to breed her to another Merino to avoid any danger of inbreeding, she still gave birth to young with faults in the female line. Of her pups, a boar and two sows, the boar took after his father (a nice sturdy Rex) but both the sows were born with cleft palates and died within a week.

Of the remaining breeds mentioned in this chapter, I own or have owned an Alpaca, a Brindle and a Harlequin. Given time, I am bound to have representatives from the rest of these breeds under my roof - you can rest assured of that. You see, I

A Harlequin.

have a speech problem: whenever a fellow enthusiast offers me one of these creatures, or an animal charity rescues one and asks me if I can take it in, I simply cannot pronounce the word, 'No'. I do try, but it always comes out, 'Oh, all right, then,' no matter how often I

resolve that I shall be strong this time and come home guinea-pig-less.

To me, a guinea pig is a guinea pig is a guinea pig, whatever its lineage. Aristocrat with a pedigree stretching back generations or mongrel that is such a mixture that it defies any form of classification - to me all pigs are equal.

A Golden Roan.

A Dalmatian guinea pig, like a Dalmatian dog, is white with black spots.

I know that I am not alone in this tendency to indulge myself in this particular way. Most of my guinea pig owning friends are the same, even those who are into the cavy show circuit in a big way. On more than one occasion, when I have been visiting one of these breeders, they have picked up one of the most mixed up parcels of guinea pig flesh I have ever set eyes upon and said something along the lines of, 'Oh, she's a total mess, but I love her to bits!'

The term 'guinea pig' has now passed into the English language to describe someone upon whom experiments, usually unpleasant ones, are carried out. The next time you pick up a guinea pig and cradle its warm soft body, treat it with the gentleness and respect it deserves, in gratitude for all that the species has done for us as we have used it for our own ends.

A Texel could be described as a Rex Sheltie.

A Tortoiseshell-and-white, positioned to show the very definite divisions of colour.

In my first two books I tried to teach people a little more about the health and husbandry of guinea pigs. This one has been far easier to put together, for I am simply trying to show their exquisite beauty. All you need to appreciate this is a pair of eyes, the sense of touch and a sense of wonder at nature's handiwork.